Growing Up Gay

Rita Reed

Growing Up Gay

The Sorrows and Joys of Gay and Lesbian Adolescence

W. W. NORTON NEW YORK • LONDON

The text and display of this book are composed in Palatino
Book design and composition by Katy Homans and Gina Webster
Layout by Rita Reed
Manufacturing by Tien Wah Press

Library of Congress Cataloging-in-Publication Data
Reed, Rita.
Growing Up Gay: The Sorrows and Joys of Gay and Lesbian Adolescence / Rita Reed.
p.   cm.
ISBN 0-393-04092-5 — **ISBN 0-393-31659-9** (pbk.)
1. Gays—United States—Biography. I. Title.
HQ75.2.R44   1997
305.9′0664—DC21   96-47379
                                               CIP
                                               Rev.

W. W. Norton & Company, Inc., 500 Fifth Avenue, New York, N.Y. 10110
http://www.wwnorton.com

W. W. Norton & Company Ltd., 10 Coptic Street, London WC1A 1PU

1 2 3 4 5 6 7 8 9 0

Contents

Acknowledgments

My thanks to Amy and Jamie for making this book possible by taking me along as they traversed one of life's most challenging passages. I am grateful for their courage, their trust in me, and the gift of their friendship. I am also indebted to Amy's parents, Jim and Sue Grahn, her sister, Alison, and brother, Chris, and to Jamie's parents, Bob and Carol Nabozny, and his two brothers, Corey and T.J. Thank you for your integrity in standing with Amy and Jamie and for your hospitality in opening your homes and lives to me.

I also express my gratitude to the many other young people who welcomed me into their community and lives. Some of you are in my photographs and all of you are in my heart. Thanks to Rusty, Lizz, Brennan, Katie, Jessey, Ken, Jennifer, Karen, Shane, Jason, Jon, Jill, Sara, Shary, Beth, Sheila, Terrance, Aaron, Julian, Chris, Sebastian, Derek, Antoine, Troy, Paul, Justin, Dan, Erin, Penny, Nikki, Michael, Kathy, Sylvia, and many others.

This work became a book only through the help and support of many good and generous people. I remain forever indebted to:

Mike Healy, supervisor, colleague, and friend, whose journalistic, picture-editing, and technical skills have aided me, from the initial project brainstorming seven years ago to last week's computer crash. Thanks for your commitment to the work and for your keen eye, your sympathetic ear, your helpful hand, and all your wise words.

Jim Mairs, my editor, for his vision in supporting the concept of this book and for his open, collaborative style which allowed the book to remain mine throughout, and finally for his expertise in polishing the whole work with an eye for its essence.

Maureen Graney, my agent, for the enthusiasm with which she handled this work and for her excellent guidance and mentoring.

Jim Foti, David Rees, Ron Meador, Brian Peterson, Susie Hopper, Brian and Mary Jo Moss, Anders Ramberg, Vickie Kettlewell, Pam Miller-Johnson, John Habich, Elaine Gale, Sally Apgar, Judy Griesedieck, and Sally Williams for reviewing various portions of the work in progress and suggesting improvements.

Nancy Andrews, for openly sharing her own book experience, and for her encouragement and our delightful camaraderie.

Leo Treadway, for his trust in opening the first door.

Kurt Chandler, my partner in the newspaper phase of the project, for his team-building, hard work, and the personal passion that he brought to this topic as he made it his own.

Joel Kramer, Tim McGuire, Darlene Pfister, Ron Meador, and Tim Bitney, editors at the *Star Tribune*, for supporting the original project.

Nikon, Inc., for the corporate support of the sabbatical grant that made possible the completion of the photographic work. Also, Bill Pekala and Carol Fisher, for their personal assistance in clearing the way for publication of the work.

Colin Covert, Jon Bream, Peter Koeleman, Dan Fenner, the lab staff, and my fellow staff photographers at the *Star Tribune* for their contributions, information, expertise, resources, and support.

Two people who played especially significant roles are no longer here for me to thank. So I thank the memory and the families of Sylvia Frisch and Howard Chapnick.

Sylvia Frisch, a former *Star Tribune* librarian, first assisted me in researching the topic. The interest, expertise, and passion she brought to the search was far more than I could have expected. Her work informs the words and pictures in this book.

Howard Chapnick, former president of Black Star, encouraged me in my dream of publishing this work as a book. His attention and assistance, especially in introducing me to Maureen Graney, helped transform the dream into reality.

Finally, I want to thank those in my life who love me and whom I love so dearly.

My mother, for her endless devotion and love. She nurtures me and forgives my exuberant excesses, from my preschool transgression of wearing red cowboy boots with a ruffled-taffeta party dress through the latest one—the publishing of this book.

My brother, Sam, for his immediate and unconditional acceptance; it has been my bulwark for years.

My father, for the gifts of comfort and ease that his affinity for my basic nature has always provided, and for the hours of *Gunsmoke* we shared.

Mary Ruth, my Sunday school teacher and confidante, for her concern and compassionate ear, especially during my adolescence.

Mark, the hometown gay boy I married and lived with for nine years, for the ballast he afforded me during my own passage and for the gifts his activism has given our community.

Mary Louise, my sweetheart, friend, and mate for life, for her constant and abiding presence and love, for her belief in me and this work, and for the support and help she has given me every day of the last seven years. She is truly the wind beneath my wings.

Introduction

A small voice whispers again and again. Who is speaking and
what is being said may not be understood for years. Then one
day they hear clearly—recognizing the voice as their own.

"Coming out" is the name gay and lesbian people give the
process of identifying, accepting, and disclosing their sexual
identity. It starts with self-recognition and ripples outward as
individuals accept themselves and risk revealing their true selves
to an ever-widening circle. It is a response of honesty, made in
the quest of becoming who they are meant to be.

Today, young people are becoming aware of and entering
this process younger than in the past. These are great acts of
courage, for it is not easy work . . . this becoming yourself in the
face of a world that wants you to be someone else. This book
documents the experiences of one boy and one girl as they pass
through the fires of this highly individual, yet nearly universal
gay and lesbian experience. It is my hope that the lives of these
two representative youngsters can reveal the humanity, the
problems, and the promise of this hidden group of minority
youth.

There is a reluctance to admit the existence of such young
people. Conventional wisdom holds that same-sex attractions are
only an adolescent phase, therefore gay teenagers do not exist
and all young people are heterosexual. This denial of the reality
in gay and lesbian kids' lives accommodates two conflicting cul-
tural beliefs—that children are innately innocent and good and
that homosexuals are inherently perverse and sinful.

This paradox is a quagmire for gay and lesbian adolescents.

At puberty, the vague inkling of difference they have felt for years manifests itself as sexual attraction to members of the same sex. But it is difficult for them, even in today's information-rich society, to find out what it means to be gay or lesbian, because the topic is rarely discussed except as social problem or controversy. Popular culture offers them few positive role models. So, in ignorance, teens wrestle with stigma and shame. They are alone in this struggle, terribly alone. Damien Martin and Emery Hetrick, founders of New York's first social service agency for gay and lesbian teens, reported that 95 percent of their clients thought they were alone, the only one who was different in this way.

The result of so much isolation is a staggering suicide rate. The *Report of the Secretary's Task Force on Youth Suicide* for the U.S. Department of Health and Human Services revealed that suicide had become epidemic among adolescents, and that gay and lesbian adolescents were two to three times more likely than their peers to attempt suicide, possibly accounting for as many as 30 percent of completed youth suicides annually. Suicide, the report informed, was the leading cause of death for gay and lesbian teenagers.

It was this 1989 study—and a radio news report about the efforts of certain U.S. senators to suppress a portion of it—that galvanized me to undertake the photographic project that eventually grew into this book. Suppression of the report seemed another turn around the vicious circle of silence and misinformation that maintains the isolation and despair leading to suicide. The injustice inherent in stifling teenagers' last cries for help was unbearable.

People need information about gay and lesbian teens. First, so that parents, educators, counselors, and other responsible adults—society in general—can begin a social discourse about meeting the needs of these teens compassionately and responsibly. And second, so that gay kids entering the tumultuous and vulnerable period of adolescence can realize that they are not really alone in their difference.

I grew up in a small Midwestern town during the 1950s and 1960s. There was no information, and no one spoke of "it." Since homosexuality was still considered psychopathological, it was best to know nothing. I could have been expelled from college, confined to a mental institution, or fired from my first job as a high school teacher if I had been suspected of homosexuality. It wasn't safe to even think about, so I didn't. I moved through adolescence and early adulthood numb—my sexuality a secret even from myself. Denial wore thin by my late twenties, and gradually I acknowledged I was a lesbian. Still, I hid my orientation, fearing if others knew who I really was, I would be ruined.

I was nearly forty before I found the courage to tell an editor, and only then because I was assigned to a story in the gay and lesbian community and wanted to be honest. I stood in the door of his office, trembling as I made my announcement. The man received my confession, thanked me for my forthrightness, and assured me that he had complete confidence in my standards, ethics, and credibility. I remain eternally grateful for his open-minded and professional response. However, I know that my feelings of release and freedom came not from his response, but from finally "coming out" at work.

It was another step on a lifelong journey to a point seven years ago, when in the midst of my ravings—that the suicide study's finding must be reported, that eyes must be opened to the lives of these kids, that someone must give body to their voices and feelings—I heard myself say: "This is yours to do."

There are many difficulties inherent in doing a book such as this. It was hard to find subjects. It took a great deal of time and effort to develop and maintain the relationships essential to photographing with intimacy and depth. The teenagers had to be willing to be seen, to be known—open enough to let a photographer spend time with them and be present during vulnerable moments. Explaining my presence sometimes required being public about their sexuality. Other gays or lesbians had to be willing to be revealed. Since the subjects, as well as their peers, were minors, parents had to sign releases.

My first opening was a calendar item in a Twin Cities gay newspaper that said, "L & G Youth Together" and offered a phone number. Leo Treadway, the adult facilitator of what turned out to be a support group for gay and lesbian teens, answered my call. After several discussions, Leo invited me to talk with the group about following one of them for a year or two to document the life of a gay teenager. The teens agreed the story was desperately needed, but none wanted to be the subject. Only one was even willing to consider it, and not if it was going to be published in his hometown newspaper.

I attended their weekly meetings for a year, listening to their problems, learning what mattered, what made them happy or sad, and, in general, what their lives were like. Always, I searched for a willing subject in whose life the fundamental issues of this group were being played out. I started photographing the one willing boy—as he moved from his home after altercations with his mother over his homosexuality.

Simultaneously, the newspaper librarian, Sylvia Frisch, and I began researching mainstream and gay media and the professional journals of educators, social workers, psychologists, and pediatricians. Information was scarce at the time, even in the gay press. The professional journals contained a smattering of studies revealing adolescence as a time of unfolding homosexual as well as heterosexual identity and establishing that gay and lesbian teens did indeed exist and were in a crisis.

A study by Jay and Young and another by Bell, Weinberg, and Hammersmith interviewed adult gays and lesbians retrospectively about adolescent experiences. Chandler Burr and Ritch C. Savin-Williams synthesized scientific studies dealing with the theoretical causes of homosexuality. Antigay violence data had been compiled and reported by Kevin Berrill. Richard Troiden outlined the stages of homosexual identity formation. The most poignant information came from people working with small populations of gay and lesbian teens in a few cities.

At New York's Hetrick-Martin Institute, first Damien Martin and Emery Hetrick and then Joyce Hunter had gleaned data and information from several thousand youngsters using the social agency's services or taking classes at the institute's school for gay and lesbian dropouts. In Minneapolis, Gary Remafedi, a physician with the Adolescent Health Program at the University of Minnesota Hospital and Clinics, was studying gay adolescents utilizing his HIV prevention program. On the West Coast, San Francisco's Larkin Street Youth Center and Huckleberry House, a runaway shelter for adolescents, reported statistics on young gays and lesbians in their client base. Virgin-ia Uribe started Project 10, a district-wide program designed to lower gay and lesbian dropout rates in the Los Angeles public schools.

The research and what I was learning from the kids all pointed in the same direction. This group of minority youth was severely isolated. The institutions—family, school, and church—that normally offer adolescents acceptance, understanding, counseling, and support are often the very sources of difficulty for young gays and lesbians.

Family is a refuge for children of ethnic minorities when they encounter racism and prejudice in society, but the gay or lesbian youth belongs to a minority that his or her parents don't belong to, and consequently feels "different" and isolated even from family. Awareness that homosexuality is a direct contradiction of the family's expectations is a source of guilt, shame, and fear of rejection. Disaster can strike when parents discover their offspring is gay or lesbian. They had expected their child to be heterosexual, so they have lost something important; in addition, they may fear that they somehow caused the homosexuality. Parents struggle through the stages of denial, anger, guilt, shame, and grief. For the adolescent such a time can be a figurative or literal abandonment by the family. Remafedi found that half of the gay adolescents he studied received a negative response from parents about their sexual orientation and that 26 percent left home during this difficult time. Joyce Hunter's review of Hetrick-Martin clients revealed that 11 percent of the youths experienced violent physical attacks at the hands of family members over sexuality. According to the federal suicide study, young gays and lesbians make up a quarter of the homeless teens on America's streets.

School can be a schizophrenic place, with educators serving up the silent treatment while peers wield a steady barrage of ostracism, slurs, harassment, and physical abuse that appears to receive the tacit approval of the adults. The organization and funding of public education binds schools to the will of the local majority, making it difficult for school officials to be open in providing information, support, or help for gay teens. A nationwide study of gay adults conducted by the National Gay and Lesbian Task Force found that nearly half of the gay men and one in five of the lesbian respondents had experienced verbal or physical assault in secondary school. Berrill reported that in a study by New York State, teenagers surveyed about their biases reacted more negatively to gay people than to any other minority group. The report concluded that gays and lesbians "are perceived as legitimate targets that can be openly attacked." In the survey of a Massachusetts high school, 97.5 percent of the students said they had heard antigay and antilesbian remarks at school, and 60 percent said they would be upset or afraid if people thought they were gay or lesbian. School becomes a hostile place that gay and lesbian teens dread and even fear. Distractions and absences lead to academic failure and school dropout.

When young gays and lesbians approach their churches seeking solace or guidance, they are more likely to receive moral cen-

ing solace or guidance, they are more likely to receive moral censure. With only a couple of exceptions, almost every religious denomination in America either openly condemns homosexuality or is involved in a rancorous internal debate about the topic. Young gays and lesbians absorb the message that they are morally tarnished—defiled by one of their own attributes.

In the face of such stigma, teens have three options—to attempt to change, to become invisible, or to be an outcast.

Young gay people try to deny, purge, or cure homosexual feelings, attractions, and fantasies, despite what Chandler Burr outlines as five decades of psychiatric evidence that sexual orientation is immutable and not susceptible to reversal. Many initiate sexual activity with members of the opposite sex in attempts to prove heterosexuality to themselves and others. Jay and Young found that 83 percent of lesbians and 66 percent of gay men have engaged in heterosexual sex. Bell and Weinberg reported almost identical numbers and added that in contrast to their heterosexual counterparts, the gays and lesbians reported such experiences as ungratifying. Martin contended that trying and failing to change often intensified feelings of self-hate and opened the door for self-destructive behaviors such as substance abuse and suicide.

If teens opt for invisibility, electing to hide or to try passing as heterosexuals, their life becomes a lie and their socialization one of deception. They pull away from family and friends for fear of being discovered. They spend more and more time alone and silently suffer fear and low self-esteem. Their social development is thwarted as they are progressively isolated from meaningful social relationships. Their risk of suicide rises. These are kids, sometimes loners, sometimes kids who appear to have everything going for them, who suddenly and seemingly inexplicably kill themselves.

If their sexuality is suspected, discovered, or openly admitted, young gays and lesbians are ostracized, ridiculed, harassed, or abused emotionally or physically at school and maybe even at home. Some are suspected because of mannerisms, attire, or attitudes that are atypical of their sex. Some are betrayed by friends whom they trusted with feelings or fears. Some are discovered during their search for information, or when they are seen in areas known to be frequented by gays, or when a gay newspaper or book is found hidden in their room or school locker. However their orientation becomes known, these teens bear the full brunt of conflicts with individuals and institutions over their homosexuality. The suicide study identifies these kids as the most likely to be pushed out of schools and families and forced to survive on their own. They face tremendous pressures, and suicide sometimes seems the only way out.

Armed with research, teen contacts, and sample photos of one gay boy forced from his home, I submitted a project proposal to Minneapolis *Star Tribune* editors. Interest in the topic had been generated by the recent murders of two gay men and the wounding of a gay teenager in the company of the second victim—a former state legislator. This news element along with strong support from several editors resulted in approval, and Kurt Chandler, an excellent reporter and a heterosexual parent with two children, was assigned to work with me. We were given a month to find subjects whose stories worked both in words and pictures.

We began by contacting the few courageous adults working with gay kids, hanging out in spots the teens frequented, going anywhere a kid invited us, and chatting on the phone for hours with dozens of adolescents. The unsolved murders that whetted the paper's appetite had just the opposite effect on possible subjects. Media reports that police suspected the murders were the work of one killer with a vendetta against gays left boys fearing they could become a target if they told their story in the newspaper. But by month's end, we had two teens, one boy and one girl, who were willing, just barely, to tell their story and who either turned eighteen before we published or had parents willing to sign a release.

Over the next seven months, teens came and went. One girl called us, interested in participating. One of the original two changed his mind after his parents threatened to disown him if he told his story in the newspaper. Another boy replaced him and then he, too, withdrew, convinced by his parents that it would kill his grandfather to learn that his grandson was gay. Yet another boy replaced him. I documented portions of the lives of ten teens during the course of the year we worked on the project, which was published as a fourteen-page special section in December 1992.

Only in the life of Amy Grahn, the girl who called us, was the struggle between succumbing to or overcoming the trauma of growing up gay playing itself out with the power of a narrative. Human development is a spiral with up-and-down and back-and-forth movements. Amy was on the cusp of claiming her identity. Sometimes she moved backward into the isolation, despair, and depression that had threatened her life once before. At other times she thrust herself forward in search of self-acceptance, friends, companionship, love, and commitment.

Amy's seeking us out after hearing about the project from another teen was an indication of her readiness to tell her story—to "come out." Her motivations were both personal and altruistic. Isolated from and ostracized and rebuked by her peers, she welcomed us as witnesses to her experience. She also wanted to help others—saying that if she just touched one person, she would be happy. For these reasons and because she made a commitment to the project, she found the strength to come out again and again when obliged to explain why a photographer was following her.

I was pleased with Amy's section of the newspaper report, but dissatisfied with my visual portrayal of gay boys. Lack of access forced me to make a composite story from several individual lives. The result seemed too stereotypical—the antithesis of my purpose. I needed to find a boy whose life was accessible and addressed issues not present in Amy's life, such as difficulties with family and the special problems of gay and lesbian adolescents in rural areas. I applied for and received the 1993 NPPA/Nikon Documentary Sabbatical grant, which allowed me to work with Amy for another year and search for the missing boy.

Within a month, I met Jamie Nabozny, a seventeen-year-old who had just arrived in the Twin Cities. He had run away from his home in Ashland, Wisconsin, to escape abuse by peers at school. Things were still tense between him and his father over his homosexuality. He wasn't ready to separate from his family, but for survival's sake he chose life alone in the big city in the hope of finding a safe place where he could fit in.

Jamie also was ready to tell his story, to protest the injustice he had undergone in public school. He hoped that if others knew his story, they would support equal treatment of gay and lesbian kids in the nation's schools. He was determined to make a difference.

Amy and Jamie found they didn't fit in the standard mold, so they began searching for and inventing their own lives. With courage, they rejected society's judgments, and in doing so they resolved the paradox about their essential nature. Through introspection, they discovered that the source of negativity was external, not internal, and they began to forge identities imbued with honesty and personal integrity.

Their courage, creativity, and willingness to be seen made this book possible. My contribution was meeting them with receptivity and openness. Our relationships started with the premise that I was a visitor to their lives. I wanted to be around as much as possible, but not without their permission. However, since we had a mutual interest—the telling of their stories—I reserved the right to argue for my presence in situations I felt essential to understanding their lives. There were only three such discussions. Once the answer remained no, and the other two times, compromise was reached and I photographed but wore earplugs.

Dependability and responsiveness were important to them, so I gave them my pager number for twenty-four-hour access and returned any call within the hour. We met or talked by phone several times a week about upcoming events, what was exciting or what was a bummer. They let me tag along to work and school and even on dates, and they allowed me just to hang out with them. We spent a great deal of time together. I waited a lot—until they finished playing video games, until someone arrived, until they decided what to do, until they actually did it, until they felt something. In time, they began keeping me informed about important events and feelings in their lives. One or the other of them would call and say, "The greatest thing is gonna happen—you've got to be here!" or "I feel terrible. I've been bawling my head off, so it must be pretty important. Thought you'd wanna know, you know, in case you wanna come over."

Gaining such access was essential for revealing the deep emotions involved in coming out. However, I had to maintain certain boundaries. Using the camera without disrupting the fabric of reality is a delicate balancing act—it is the challenge of documentary photography. I had to enter the authentic relationships that undergird making emotionally intimate photographs, yet, at the same time, minimize the effect of my presence on the course of their lives. I adhere to the adage "Change nothing and do no harm." So, for example, I rode the bus or walked with them rather than give them a ride, and when problems arose, I tried to be a good listener, without offering input or advice.

I worked close with short lenses. If I tried working farther away with a long lens, it felt awkward to Jamie and Amy—like being observed. They wanted me to step into the stream of their lives, and at times it felt almost like dancing, moving around them, swirling in time, the shutter opening and closing . . . opening and closing . . . selecting fractions of seconds from their lives and suspending them as photographs. I hope that as you view them and read what Amy and Jamie have to say about their lives, you will truly meet these two young people. I ask that you bring what they asked of me—the receptivity of an open heart and mind.

If you are a parent, a brother or sister, a schoolmate, a teacher, or a concerned adult—may you find new understanding and appreciation of your child, your sibling, your classmate, your student, or the kid next door.

If you are a gay or lesbian person of an earlier generation—may you retrieve, as did I, a sweet remnant of a missed or lost adolescence.

If you are a young person just discovering your sexual orientation— may you see that while it takes courage and creativity, your life is a great joy waiting for you to live it.

Amy Grahn

Introduction

The changes began when I came back my eighth-grade year. I thought that I had some pretty cool friends in seventh grade, but in eighth grade I realized I didn't because they didn't respect me for who I was really. I guess I've always been kind of a tomboy, and in seventh grade I changed. I did that junior high thing . . . tried to be like everybody else. It was that makeup thing, yeah, I tried to conform and fit in.

But I didn't like it. I realized I just wanted to be me and wear jeans and feel however I wanted to feel, be comfortable. They just stopped hanging out with me when I was more myself.

There was nothing that happened that should have made them disappear, they just did. I tried to find out what was going on, to talk to them, but they were just so weird. I can't even explain it. I was just treated way differently. I just knew that it was over and we weren't friends.

A boy in my math class wrote me a note asking me if I had a penis or if I thought I had a penis or something like that. It really upset me and I gave it to the school counselor. The boy got suspended for a couple of days. My school counselor recommended me to West Suburban Teen Clinic and I started seeing a therapist. The first time I saw her I couldn't stop shaking.

I felt really alone and different, like an outcast, I guess. I got to thinking, why even be here if I'm not going to have any friends. One day, I called my therapist, Pam, and told her I didn't want to live anymore and that I was going to the garage and hang myself. She immediately called my mom and dad and before I had a chance to, I was locked away.

I went into a hospital, a mental institution. I was there for a week and a half and then I got let out and started in a day program. That wasn't working, I got depressed again and was doing bad things, like carving "L.S." for "Life Sucks" on my arms with razor blades. They put me back in again. After I got out that time, I went to Delta Place. I was there for eleven months and I learned to accept me and have a higher self esteem.

When I was fifteen years old, Pam asked me to make a list of things I wanted to talk about in counseling. The top thing on my list was sexuality. It was the only word I had. I said I want to talk about this topic—help me understand what it means. I knew this word was an issue in me. That's like when I wrote it down and I knew. I probably knew before but I didn't. It was subconscious before, I think.

We talked about if I was going to tell my parents . . . I was scared to tell 'em. What would my parents think? We didn't know anybody like that, so I automatically thought that I was completely weird. So why would they want this strange daughter, who did strange things, you know? I had no idea what they would do. They might have kicked me out or something like that. They would disown me. That's what I really thought.

It was just a fear because it was never talked about. I didn't know anybody. I never knew anybody that was different like me. I can honestly say I never knew anybody who was gay when I was little. Kids would say things at school—you know how kids are, faggot, lesbo, that kind of thing, you know, and it's all derogatory. So immediately you think that it's bad. I thought that I was by myself. I thought I was a freak.

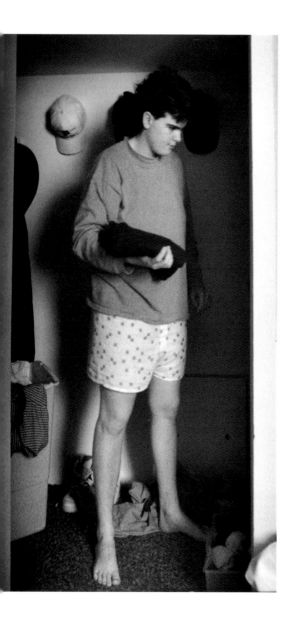

I was so different from all the other girls—I really was—the way I dressed, you know. My dad tried to make a rule when I was in grade school, that I would wear a dress once a week to school. I said forget that idea. That's not happening here, you know. No way was I going to wear a dress to school. It wasn't me. I didn't feel comfortable.

I usually ate by myself. I didn't like this whole cafeteria lunch thing, I felt like I'd walk in there and everybody would be looking at me. Even at South I hated it.

I went to South in the city my sophomore year because they had a gay and lesbian group. But I had to get up so ungodly early to ride in with my dad. It got very tiresome. I was worn out. I thought, I'm in the eleventh grade, I'll give Minnetonka a try again, maybe it will work better. It didn't.

Nobody on the basketball team gave me problems, they just didn't include me. They had parties after games. I didn't get invited and I felt pretty rotten about it.

It's that suburban thing. I was different from what they think is normal. I mean, look at me, it's quite evident that I'm not the picture-perfect woman from Minnetonka. You know they were raised where women are supposed to look like . . . this . . . this . . . feminine. You know, have your makeup on and big hair. It's so unnatural. I don't know what else to say about it, it's just really the stinkers. It stinks. But everybody I know does it. My mom is like that. She's the traditional housewife who wears her makeup because she thinks she looks better. That's the way society makes women feel. It's all just a big game.

My parents got Snoopy when I was in the hospital . . . so my sister and I had a friend . . . somebody who would love us unconditionally.

I hadn't given my parents much credit. I pushed myself away when I went through all that stuff. I didn't want to be close to them. I didn't want their help.

Then . . . my mom . . . her exact words were, "Your dad and I are wondering if you're dealing with your sexuality."

I said, "No," and went to my room. I was upset. I knew that I was having sexuality issues . . . that I was very attracted to women. I didn't want her to know, no way.

I came back out five minutes later and said, "Yes, and so what if I am?"

Their response was positive. It was like, we love you, no matter what. From that moment it's been nothing but support from them. I underestimated my parents when I didn't want to tell them.

Me and my dad goof around and I can talk to him about pretty much anything. He has this alter ego Jerry—his evil twin brother. Jerry talks funny, makes really crazy faces at people in other cars, goofy stuff. Jerry causes lots of trouble. If he knew I was having a down day, he'd try to make me laugh. Jerry really helped me out a lot of times, lifted me right out of the hole.

If Dad's mad, he'll let me know. He might not talk to me for a while. Then he'll sit down and write things down—make it so I can see what I can do about it. My mom is more the fix-it kind. Mom tells me what she thinks and what she thinks I should do to solve a problem.

Uh oh, Mom's disgusted with me for some reason. Once my mom starts crying, there's no stopping me. I lose it. I just start to feel real bad and I start to cry too. It's crazy how we're connected like that.

We got to be altar girls when the new priest came; the old one wasn't as open-minded. I always thought it would be cool, but then it got old. My family wasn't really religious, but we went to church every Sunday and a lot of our values were based on the church. I don't like the church. Maybe I'm rebelling from my parents in a way. You know, how do I know that it's really my belief and not just theirs?

My brother couldn't stay at girls' houses and I couldn't stay at boys' houses, you know. So then we all figured out I was a lesbian, and they didn't know where to go with this issue about me staying at girls' houses because all my friends were girls and I was dating girls. It was confusing for them. It ended up that I could stay at girls' houses, but my parents had to meet them once. When girls came to my house, they had to sleep in a totally separate room.

I was sleeping over at some friends', Jen and Karin, and we ended up going to a crazy party at Katie Palmer's. I probably got sloshed. It was the fun I never got to have. No mom and dad to tell me to stop doing that. Don't drink that much. I just felt really comfortable and like I could be myself.

The next day I went over there again, hung out with her, and we ended up going to coffee at the Café Wyrd. I think it was a date. I'm not sure if she thought of it that way or not.

I was seventeen and she was twenty-three. I thought it was cool that she was an older woman. I pushed and made the first move. I wanted to kiss her, so I did.

I really didn't know very many lesbians—only the five at the group I went to. That's where I'd met Jen and Karin. Katie was fun, we partied, hung out with crazy people, got drunk. We were social.

This was my best birthday ever. My mom surprised me, which was great. Katie and my best friend, Jen, were there. They told me they couldn't come for some stupid reason. Then all of sudden they were there. I was as happy as a lark. At dinner my dad told that joke.

"Did you hear about the new line of tennis shoes for lesbians? Dykies, but they had to be recalled. The tongues weren't long enough."

Katie and Jen and Karin thought it was hilarious. I thought my dad was hip. All right, Dad!

I turned eighteen, and could go to some of the bars. I felt just like I belonged there, like I really fit in and could have fun dancing and meeting people. This is really when my social life began to change. Yeah, things definitely took a turn for the better.

I hate it when people stare, you know. My mom taught me not to stare because it's rude. It happens to this day and it drives me crazy.

People used to stare at me when I'd go into the women's bathroom when I was a kid. One woman pointed at the sign on the door and said, "This is the ladies' room." I said, "I know." I just hated it, you know. I thought, why don't people know that I'm a girl? You know, I think I have a woman's face.

Sometimes I felt kind of embarrassed, but at the same time I don't really care. It was just all a bunch of mixed feelings. To this day, I hate going into the women's bathroom.

It's not a new thing to me to have people stare at me—look me up and down because I'm different.

I dated Katie for three weeks and she helped me expand my involvement with the community—just by going places with her and meeting all the people that she knew. Then I wanted to date other people, because now I knew more, and there were more possibilities.

I felt like I needed space. Which later I thought was the biggest mistake I ever made, 'cause I wanted her back. Probably because I saw her with someone else. I hated that. Here I wanted to see other people, but I just hated it that she was. Gosh!

Her house in the city was like my second home. It was a hangout—a place where I went when I skipped school or didn't go to work.

I guess I was just afraid that I was going be alone, you know—again. That I would just not be important anymore. I didn't want to lose the people I had met through her because we weren't going to be together anymore.

I found out about rugby from a woman who worked at Café Wyrd. I ended up going and trying out. I played for two seasons. My nickname was Peewee, because I was the youngest player on the team. I'm not really small. I'm five nine and a half and pretty big. I became more and more muscular as I played with them.

I liked the physicalness of the sport. When we scrum, oh boy! The three in the front row lock together and then us second-row people lock. Our heads go between the bodies of the front-row women and our hands go between their legs and grab [the waistbands of] their shorts. The ball's thrown in the middle and you push. The idea is to have the ball come out behind your team—to get possession of it. The eight-man kicks it out behind and the flyhalf gets the ball and passes it off to the backs, who run it up the field, they're the quick ones.

We were playing in the Midwest Women's Rugby Tournament in Chicago. When their secondman jumped up to get the throw-in, I just nailed her—plastered her to the grass. I loved it. I mean, it was an awesome hit, a high moment. I felt big! Inside, in who I was, I felt big. I don't know what it was, though. Partly the people, and that they just accepted me and worked with me to really learn what I was doing and make me good. It's amazing what getting to know people who are like you and accept you does to you.

I liked the road trips. Camaraderie, is it called camaraderie? I liked going to places like Chicago and playing rival teams, but I also liked going out afterwards to a different bar and just hanging out and meeting the other teams and bonding with my teammates.

At the end of the tournament, there was this huge party at a bar and they had this Miss Something-or-other contest. It kind of spoofed beauty pageants. It was a talent show and this Michigan woman got up and did this body-shot thing to one of the judges.

First, Miss Michigan pours salt on the judge's neck and puts a lime in between the judge's teeth. Then she licks her neck, drinks a shot of tequila, and takes the lime out of the judge's mouth with her mouth. It's a sexual thing, you know. I'd never seen anything like it before. Wow!

I'd gone to Gay Pride the year before, but I wasn't sure about it all. I didn't march. This year was different. My mother and sister marched with P-FLAG. I felt a lot different, just knowing my family wanted to make an effort to really be a part of my life, no matter what it was. I felt much more involved. I felt like I was a part of it. I wasn't just watching it, checking it out. Now I knew this is what I wanted to do.

It felt like I was proclaiming something. That I was telling everybody, and I was okay with that . . . it's funny how I like myself when I never used to. Now I'm telling however many thousands of people that are there—it was very public. I think it was an important step for me. I felt very connected, overwhelmed with all these homosexuals all in the same place at one time. It was exhilarating. It's our day.

I felt really stuck, so far away from the city and the people I wanted to hang out with. It was really frustrating. There were always restrictions on the car. I could only take it to the cities twice a week. It wasn't enough for me. No way! I had to be home by midnight. I hated that. I wanted to stay out and party.

I was skipping school. Even though I was back at South my senior year, I hated it. I was so over school, so done. I didn't have any friends there. All my friends were out of school. Sheila was a rugby buddy. She knew I was wanting to move out, so she offered to let me live with her.

I moved out when my mom was in Florida. I called her and she asked me to wait until she got back. I didn't want to. I made sure I left when nobody was home. My dad didn't agree with what I was doing.

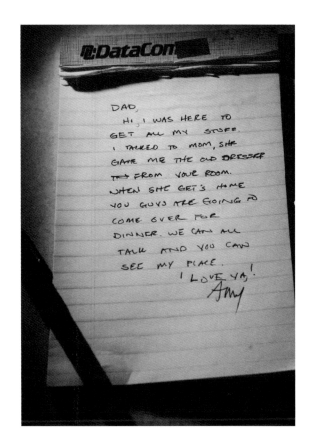

I'm feeling pretty cool. I'm on my own turf, my own pad, you know. It's definitely a different feeling, very exhilarating.

It was mine, in a house where I didn't have anybody to tell me what to do. I could bring whoever I wanted home and they could sleep with me in my damn bed . . . and my parents couldn't tell me that it wasn't okay. I could play music loud if I wanted to. I mean, not obnoxiously loud or anything.

My rooms always looked the same, no matter where I moved. I always have this way I like things to be. I'm very particular. In my room I like it neat and organized.

They were a cool group of women. They liked to do fun things, you know, party a little. We went to the bars together. Every Wednesday at a certain time, a bunch of us met down at the park to shoot hoops. We'd hang out at the coffee shops and go bike riding every once in a while.

I went to school some days, but most days I just wouldn't get up. Sheila actually tried to get me to go. She would tell me that I needed to go to school.

School wasn't fun. The only class that I ever liked was science, because the teacher made it so interesting that I got an A. It's hard for me to sit still and listen for a whole hour; I begin to fall asleep. I tend to learn better when I'm doing. I'm more of a hands-on kind of person.

Not long after I moved, I dropped out of school halfway through my senior year. I got a telemarketing job—selling siding and gutters.

They wanted to go rock climbing and I was supposed to work. But I didn't go—called in sick, quit or something—irresponsible.

It just felt great to be outside doing something that I enjoyed. I like rock climbing, the physicality, the challenge. It was a different kind of challenge than rugby. To go from the bottom to the top, to climb it. To find the little space to grab onto to pull yourself up to the next spot. It was very challenging. It was an individual thing. They might have been down at the bottom and said, "To your left, there's a great spot." But it was definitely more me.

I didn't always make it up the first time. I would get halfway up and I couldn't go farther, so I'd come back down and I'd try it again. So when I got to the top, it was a bigger accomplishment for myself, because I did it alone. I felt like I really did something.

I was such a player! I dated a lot of girls. I liked the attention. I think I was starved for somebody to love me.

These girls were all over me all night. I thought it was great that these women just wanted me, but they weren't my type at all. Too femmie! I mean, I kinda like a butch girl.

I slept with women hoping that every one would work out, but none of them did. Yeah, that was a crazy time, but then I met Lizz and it changed.

Lizz was fun, I liked her personality. She wasn't like the bar people, who drank all the time. Lizz is a college student, wants to become a doctor, she doesn't drink. She's never been with anybody. I was her first girlfriend.

I'd call and she'd say, "I wish you were here." I'd rollerblade to the dorm and call her from downstairs. She'd say, "What are you doin'?" I'd say, "I'm sittin' downstairs." She would go, "Ahhck!" I just loved to surprise her.

Our first kiss was in this bed. We were watching *Father of the Bride* and *Fern Gully*, the cartoon.

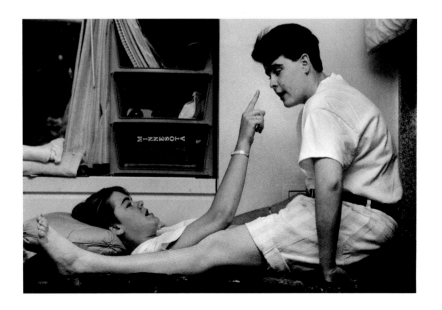

Lizz and I were still just dating. We hadn't dated all that long, a month and a half. I guess that's a fair amount of time, but we didn't have any commitment. I didn't want a commitment, and I don't think she did.

She was mad at me 'cause I got on the phone with some woman. I was talkin' to Mary.

I was going to leave and go hang out with her and then Ann called and said she was coming over to say goodbye to Lizz. School was over and Lizz's parents were movin' her home in the morning.

I wanted to see Ann, 'cause Ann's a groovy gal. She lived out by my parents, in Orono or something—close.

She was straight, I thought.
Lizz didn't think she was, but
I did, kind of—kind of not.
Yeah, I thought Ann was cool,
that's all I felt towards Ann.
I think Lizz thought I had a
crush on her. I thought Ann
was cute, but that was it. I
didn't want anything from her.
I thought Lizz liked Ann.

Everybody was coming over to say goodbye. Dan was there, too. Lizz had a thing with him before I met her. He kinda instigated our first date. Dan and Lizz went to the Saloon a lot—to dance. The night we met I was standing there being the butch thing that I often was at the Saloon—you know, standing just a certain way, being tough and not smiling. I was doing that all night and she was lookin' at me and watching me dance. When the bar closed, some friends came up and said that she'd been wanting to meet me all night. So, I met her. She was sitting in the front seat of the car. Dan was in the backseat. He said that she wanted to go out with me sometime. I said we could go out the next night.

I used to get jealous of Dan, actually, because I knew she slept with him and that just kind of—I just don't like hangin' out with them. I just feel real uncomfortable.

We finally slid in between the sheets to sleep together on the last night. I was ready to be like all cuddly and sexual with her, but she wanted nothing to do with that at all. She was leaving and she was stressed out about having to deal with her parents in the morning and about not being able to see me for a long time. Nothing happened. She was far too sad.

I didn't want to wake up on this day—'cause I knew she'd be gone and I was really sad about it. Her mom called real early. That's why she's draggin' me out of bed, 'cause I had to leave before they got there, 'cause they didn't know about me. Boy!

I didn't want her to go. I was losing something great that I'd found. And, well, I knew I would see her again, but I just wanted it to be the same as it always was. I didn't want it to change. I liked the dorm room. I wished we could have lived in there forever. Because things were just fun and it was like our own little world for a while. We were so into each other and it was new and wonderful and all that good stuff.

Those doors shut and she was gone, and in a way, my little world just ended. I don't like saying goodbye.

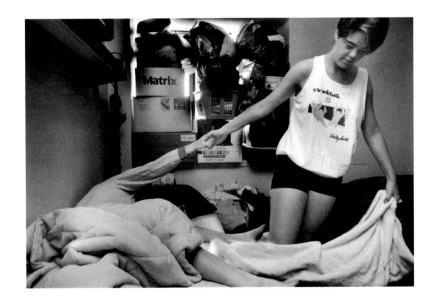

We had to camp because I wasn't welcome at her parents' house. Everything got all messed up when I visited the first time after she moved home for the summer. We were downstairs in her bedroom smoochin' and her dad came down to get a beer. The door was open and he saw us. He went upstairs and slammed the door. Lizz went up after him. I sat downstairs all stressed out, ready to cry 'cause I didn't know what to do.

Her parents didn't want me in their house so she took me to a friend's house and went back to talk with her mom and dad. She was real upset when she came back later and stayed there with me that night. We decided after the whole parents blowout thing to just see each other—to be monogamous.

We rented a boat and rowed out to the middle of the lake. We were out there a long time. I didn't care about sun, she did. I'm not a sun person. I like water, it's so peaceful. I thought it'd be fun, and it would be more private.

There were a lot of people there that day, and they were all on the beaches. It wasn't private on the beach. I felt more comfortable being close to her when we were by ourselves than with other people—so I could flirt with her, talk to her silly or just be lovey, I guess.

Also, I was nervous, that we'd have a big problem with somebody or some kind of confrontation or something like that. I sure didn't want to, like, run into her mom or dad.

I always hated to leave when I went to visit. I allowed myself to really care about her. I just fell for her. I love her.

Love is something that we all need and want and nothing can stop us from trying to find it. We keep searching for something. We don't know what it is, but we need it or we want it or we want to experience it or whatever.

One weekend when she came to see me that summer, we made love and I cried. It was the first time that ever happened. It was an incredible feeling. I didn't know what to do with it. It was kind of overwhelming, but it was wonderful.

I don't think there is any other way to describe it. You just have to feel it. You don't fully understand it until you experience both—just having sex and really being with somebody that you love.

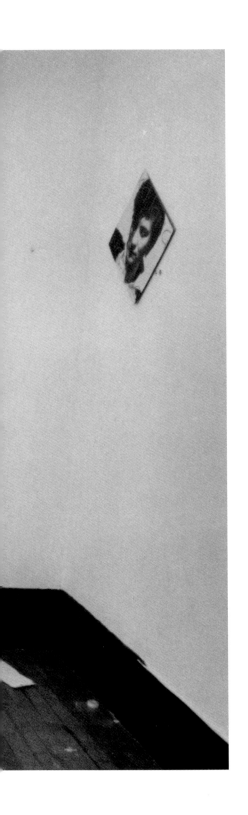

I called Lizz. I missed her incredibly and I had all these big money problems. Things just weren't working out and I was stressed out about rent. She said it wouldn't be such a bad thing to move back home. I felt like I'd be failing, or saying that I can't do it by myself, but I couldn't.

So I called Mom and said I missed Lizz and I couldn't handle being so far away from her. My mom said that when my dad went away on business, she would sometimes cry and cry. It felt good to talk to her and here I thought Mom would never understand my relationships.

My parents said, "If you're going to live in this house, you need to finish your schooling."

I contemplated going back to Minnetonka to get that high school diploma, but I decided that I couldn't do it. I needed to work, to pay these huge bills I had gotten myself into. So, I got my GED [graduate equivalency diploma]. It might not have been completing high school, but I was pretty happy.

I thought it was great that they had this ceremony for anybody who had gotten their GED through the Hopkins Community Center, but I hated it that my tassel said 1994. I completed the tests in '93 and I wanted '93 on my tassel because that was the year I was supposed to graduate.

If I could change anything now, I wish I'd gone back to school—stayed at South until I graduated.

Jamie Nabozny

Introduction

I knew from an early age that I was different. In kindergarten we played house and, like, the model was—man marries woman and they have kids. The strange thing was I wanted to marry a man, but I didn't want to be the woman. It was confusing, and lots of the times I ended up playing the mother, just so I could be married to the man. That seemed okay in kindergarten, but as I got older people didn't think it was okay anymore.

When I was seven, my uncle brought his partner home for Thanksgiving. The family talked about them behind their backs . . . about how they lived together, were kind of married, and that they were homosexuals. I was in the other room, but I could hear what they were saying, and it made a lot of sense to me. I kind of figured that I was that.

I met Jessey, my best friend, when I was twelve and he was eleven. We both were so relieved to finally talk to someone about it. We talked about guys, created a fantasy world for ourselves, bought those teen-beat magazines, and cut out the pictures of boys. I felt as if the black-and-white world I had lived in was now alive with color. Someone else finally shared my secret.

In the seventh grade . . . people said I walked like a girl. They called me fag, queer, homo. It escalated to pushing me around in the locker room, you know, telling me to quit looking at them when we were changing, that kind of stuff. I was telling the guidance counselor about it and she called a meeting with some of the kids and called their parents, so I had to tell my parents. I just said that kids were calling me names and that the guidance counselor was taking care of it. I didn't tell them what kids were calling me. I was really ashamed and embarrassed. I became more and more depressed . . . just staying in my room a lot, withdrawing from the family—not talking.

I'd confided in my aunt that I was gay and that I wanted to change. My parents sent me to live there 'cause she could home-school me, and I wouldn't have to deal with the kids anymore. I think my mom feared that I was gay and sent me to my aunt and uncle, because they were religious.

We'd pray about me being gay every night. It was really getting very difficult to be there and I just felt like I was this big old
pervert. I ran away, back to my parents' house, to tell my mom I
didn't want to be there anymore.

My aunt called the police, and that got the juvenile officer
involved. He asked Jessey what was bothering me. Jessey shared
our secret. So in front of my parents, social worker, and Al-A-
Teen sponsor, the police officer came right out and asked me if I
was gay. I said yes. My mom said she loved me and it didn't
matter but my dad had a much harder time. He was crying, both
my parents were crying, but my dad got up and left. The only

thing he said was, "It's just a stage you're in, you'll grow out of it." I felt like I was sitting there naked. Nobody wanted to talk about it after that day. My parents especially didn't want my brothers to know. I felt like I had become contagious.

I finished the seventh grade in Catholic school, but went back to public school in the eighth grade. There was physical stuff—pushing my books out of my hands, kicking, tripping. I came home from school after a really bad day, went to my room, shut my door, and just cried and cried and cried. I just couldn't see going through what I'd been going through for four more years, plus the rest of the eighth grade. I mean, that's an eternity. I thought I had a couple of choices. I could run away or I could kill myself. I thought about two things when I tried to kill myself: either that somebody would realize that I needed help and get it for me and I'd be able to leave the school, or I'd just die and it would be over with. So I took a whole bunch of pills—everything in the medicine cabinet. They pumped my stomach—I had to swallow syrup and stuff.

I tried to kill myself again early in the ninth grade, so my parents put me with another aunt and uncle so I could go to a different school district. The school was better, but my aunt and uncle weren't. They had a big-time problem with me being gay. We had a fight and the next night I ran away again, this time with Jessey. We hitchhiked all the way to Minneapolis and hid out for three weeks. My parents made up a missing-child poster and came looking for me. When I saw that poster, I started bawling. I was homesick and I really missed my parents. I wanted to go home on the agreement that I wouldn't have to go back to school.

We got back to Ashland and checked schooling options. There were none. We got a letter saying I had to go back to school or else my parents had to go to jail. I went back . . . I didn't have any other choice.

Everybody knew I ran away with Jessey. Even the girls asked, "Are you guys gay?" I said, "Yes, I'm gay." I thought if I told

them, maybe they would leave me alone because they'd finally know, and maybe it would be no big deal. But that didn't work. It got a lot worse. People threw things—pencils, nuts and bolts— at me on the school bus. I started walking to school. I was kicked, shoved. Kids made demeaning gestures and spit on me. The thing that hurt the worst was being thrown on the bathroom floor and urinated on. I'll never forget that.

I tried to kill myself again. When I got out of the hospital, the judge made Social Services send me to a treatment center—a boys' home. I was there that summer and half of my tenth-grade year. I got a lot more comfortable with myself. My counselor helped me to be proud of and basically love myself. I re–came out to my parents, because for two years I had been telling them I was straight and was going to church and everything.

When I came back to school I knew I was protected by Wisconsin law, so I reported every incident. I felt I wasn't the scum of the earth that everyone could walk all over anymore. I formed a Gay and Lesbian Youth Group. I may have been the only member, but it was there in my town of nine thousand people.

One morning, before the start of school in the eleventh grade, eight or nine boys circled me in the hall. One of them kicked me in the stomach again and again . . . the others laughed. A few days later I had abdominal surgery. I went to school off and on after that. I just couldn't deal with it anymore. Going to school was like the hugest effort—just to get there and survive the day.

I needed to be in a safer place. I was up all night and I figured out what to do. I didn't have any money, but I had a checkbook, so early in the morning, when the diners opened, I walked downtown. At every open place I'd order and write a check for ten or twenty dollars over. I got about a hundred and twenty dollars. I thought about going to Milwaukee or Chicago—any big city. I got to the bus station—the cheapest was the Twin Cities—it cost like thirty dollars for the bus ticket and I was gone.

When I got off the bus, I was very afraid. People were passed out in the station and others were asking for money. My biggest fear was that I'd be hungry—like homeless and hungry. The major thing I didn't want was to have to be a prostitute to survive. I always said that if I was hungry or if I had to sell myself to survive I would go home. There wouldn't be a question about it.

I stayed quite a few places. I mean, I'd meet somebody and he'd say, "You want to stay at my house?" I'd say, "Sure," and I'd stay there a couple of days. Then I'd be at another place for a couple of days . . . I was here and there.

By Christmas I was really homesick. I called my mom. She was crying and happy that I called. I said: "This is the way it is. Either you let me come home for the holidays and let me move back down here afterwards or you won't see me until I turn eighteen." She agreed and they came to get me. In January, I moved to the city for good.

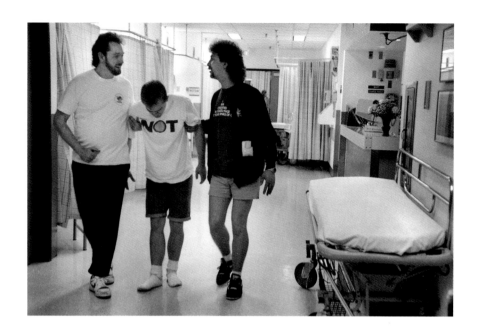

I had the idea of finding a gay foster home. I wanted to go back to school and I wanted role models—not to teach me how to be gay, but to teach me about relationships and how the whole thing worked.

I found out that Metropolitan Community Church had a lot of gay couples. I went there and met Luke and Steve. They had just bought a house with two lesbians, Pam and Nancy. They were all very involved with the church. That had once been a big part of my life, and then it wasn't because I was gay. I thought, wow, I can put those two things together.

They called my parents that same night and everything seemed to click, so I went there. It was a huge relief. I thought that it was going to be like the gay Waltons or something. I thought we'd all get along and go to bed saying "'Night, Jamie," "'Night, Auntie Em."

I learned a lot about being gay from the guys. We talked about gay sex, about being gay in a different time period—before AIDS and stuff. And about the gay community and Gay Pride celebrations. And about household stuff like laundry, cooking, setting the table.

They both cooked really well. It was all "la femme" and "la bouche" and they even had a way of setting the table. I had to learn exactly how the napkins and the plates went, the order of all the silverware and where the glasses sat—if it was long table, how the two centerpieces were centered between which plates. It just seemed so crazy to me.

I learned a lot about relationships from the girls. When I brought my first date home for Luke's birthday party, the girls were telling him things about me, making jokes about me, asking him questions—like my mom would have. I just kind of sat there and was embarrassed about it all.

The guys were able to be gay and it was okay. They were somewhat closeted, you know, they wouldn't kiss in public. It was part of how old they were. The first time I seen 'em kiss and be affectionate, it was very odd to me. I remember calling home and telling my mom how strange it was. I realized, though . . . I must look the same way when I do it.

There was always a lot of joking around—Steve was hilarious. I mean, sex was a joke. You'd say something totally not sexual and all of sudden people would laugh and it was a joke. It seems like there is a lot of joking around in the gay community. People say it is because of how much pain there is in the gay community and that humor is a really good way to deal with it.

The guys bought these "foofy" pink, lacy, low-cut seventyish-type jumpsuits. They got heels and earrings and necklaces to match. At the party we all went upstairs and they got into their matching outfits and I put on this dress of Pam's and a pair of her shoes and then we strolled down the stairs. We said these were our outfits for Pam and Nancy's wedding. It was a joke because we were all really going to wear tuxes. This was the first time I ever did drag in front of a group of people.

It was just fun. I thought we were kind of making fun of the fact that straight people have all these roles. I understood that there were drag queens but I had no clue what part they had in the community. I used to think they were like radical and were going to make us all look bad. Now I think they're kinda like heroes in a way. Especially the ones who have been around for thirty or forty years. They were like the beginning of the civil rights movement with Stonewall and stuff.

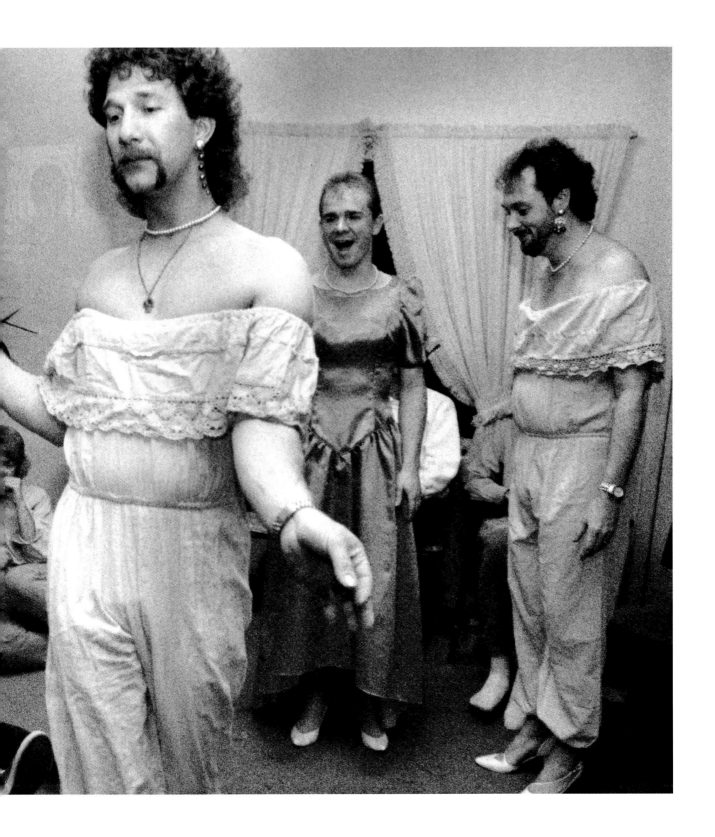

I was very honored to be in the girls' wedding. Very honored! They were like role models for me to see what I wanted. The affection I'd had in my life up to that point was very short and it wasn't really affection—it was more sex. I had the really unique opportunity to be around people who were in church and had long-term relationships, you know, had like what society would call a normal relationship.

Theirs was one of the healthiest gay relationships that I've like ever been around or experienced. I loved how in touch they were with their own feelings, how they communicated and interacted with each other, how they lived and the way they expressed their love to each other.

It was the most beautiful wedding I've ever been to in my whole life. I never cried at a wedding before and I was bawling—they were just so beautiful, the expressions on their faces.

The situation with the guys wasn't everything that I wanted it to be. Luke always criticized, scrutinized, and put me down. It seemed like a competition between us. Nothing I did was good enough—he could always do it better. I couldn't do anything right, and if I did, it wasn't right enough or good enough. Luke was really sarcastic. I ended up confronting him and it really backfired. He was really mad at me.

I paid rent, my own car payment and insurance, worked full-time, went to school, and did most of the housework—at least I thought so. It was never enough. The housework was never done right. I was gone too much. I was never home. My curfew—nine or ten—the fact that I couldn't date anyone older than myself—it was ridiculous.

I know there have to be rules, but I felt like they wanted a twelve-year-old so they could raise him, discipline him, and all this stuff. I was already grown up and beyond where I needed all the discipline, rules, and structure.

When I left Luke and Steve's, I called Tim. I was sleeping on his couch when I found the guys. He said I could stay at his place again, so me and Homer packed up and moved.

Homer is the stuffed animal that I've had since my first birthday. I could never lose Homer. When I was like ten, my dad thought I was getting too old to have a teddy bear and he threw Homer away. But I somehow knew that Homer was in the dumpster! I went out there and dug him out and cleaned him off. I had to hide him, but then my dad got used to the idea of me keeping him—as long as I didn't sleep with him.

When I'm not stationary, Homer lives in a box, but when I have a place he's on my bed. Homer has been there through all my problems, he knows them all. If he could only talk.

In the morning I faced the reality that I was homeless once again.

I wanted to find a boyfriend more than anything. I was very alone. I knew I had these feelings, but I could never express them to anyone.

When I was living with Tim I went to my first gay party ever, and I met two guys. One of them went to the same school I did. He gave me his number. I thought the other one was much more attractive, so I started dating him.

I brought him home. It was kinda nice to be in my hometown where I had longed so much just to have a boyfriend and now to find one and bring him back there. It was really important to me to show him the parts of my town that are still okay. For me the ore dock is really special place, I went there a lot as a kid. It's this huge, very masculine structure, it's really beautiful, I think. Some people wouldn't think so, but I do and I love going there.

It was a big event in my life—the first time I took a boyfriend home to meet my parents. I remember how weird it was. It was not good at all . . . Oh, they didn't like him, he was too effeminate.

My mom tried to be understanding and happy I had a boyfriend, but she had a difficult time, and my dad—my dad had a very difficult time with everything. I could tell by the way he looked at me, the way he acted and the things he said—very blunt things that were uncomfortable for both of us. Stuff about how they didn't want us kissing in front of them or in front of my brothers or especially in the town. They didn't want people to know that he was my boyfriend and that kind of stuff.

Truth is, my parents had to get over me being gay, but my grandpa never had to get over anything. I was Jamie and that was the way it was. I was up the earliest because I was walking to school, so I'd get him coffee and we'd sit and talk—about really superficial things, but there was this kind of bond there anyway. He knew I was gay and it didn't matter to him one iota, as he would say.

In one of my last visits, I told him I loved him and he said, "Remember, no matter what anybody says, you're a good boy." It was the last thing he told me.

When I'm on Lake Superior—I mean like totally out there—I get butch, very adventurous. I just knew that this wasn't for my boyfriend. It was the last place in the whole world he wanted to be. He had to walk barefoot and the rocks were hurting his feet. I'm like, "Hey! Baby!" This was the beginning of the end of our relationship. I mean, I wanted somebody who'd be able to walk through these rocks with me. These rocks are no big thing.

Things ended fast when I found out he still lived with his boyfriend. They slept in the same bed, but they both saw other people. He called it an open relationship. Like that day, I called Brennan, the other guy I met at that same party.

We went on our first date and had a lot of fun. Most people I run into aren't as out as I am, but Brennan is. His family knows and it's so open, it's really wonderful.

Brennan and I come from the same kind of family background. Being at his house is like being at home. He's like someone from my hometown—listens to country music. He says he has met Mr. Right—me. Yeah, there's competition stuff, too, but it's more playful competition than anything.

I had a permanent boyfriend. By Gay Pride week, everything was going great!

He was my first true love. Being close to him felt better than anything I've ever felt. It was the first time in my whole life that I knew somebody was in my life who cared a lot about me, not because I was their son or I was a relative, but because of who I was. He liked me for who I was, not for any other reason.

We've decided about names. He wants to keep his name because he's the only one to pass on his family name. I'm going to drop my last name and we'll combine my middle and his last name. We'll be the Stuart-Hannons.

I grew up on Lake Superior. I love the water—it's very beautiful. I wanted to share that with him. This part of the lake is really important to me. When I was a kid, I'd go down there and nobody would be able to find me. I could hide out. Down there, not much is manmade. It's very natural, it's very masculine.

But I saw another side of Brennan that I'd never seen before. He didn't like the fact that the waves were so strong. The water is not a very scary thing to me, but to him it was terrifying. In a lot of ways I didn't understand it, so I didn't respect it. Like he was afraid and I laughed, because it seemed ridiculous to be afraid of something that I thought was a lot of fun. It showed me that he was human, though. For the first time in our relationship, it made me want to take care of him, instead of him taking care of me. I remember feeling very, very close, lying on the beach holding each other and thinking how I'd love to still have this twenty years from now. Wanting not to ever have to leave.

It was exciting and scary taking Brennan to the family reunion. Scary because I didn't know how people were going to react and I thought maybe there would be arguments. You know, that somebody would say how I don't belong there or how he doesn't belong there or something. I wanted, you know, to make sure that he felt accepted and all that stuff. It went way better that I thought it would. Everybody knew who and what he was and nobody cared.

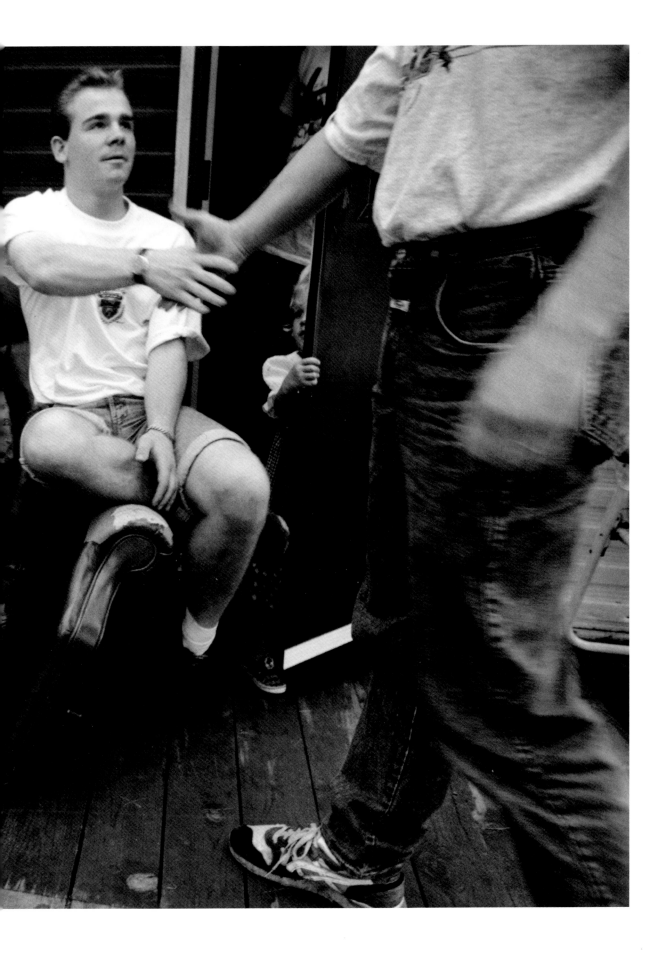

It was kind of a weird thing. Brennan wasn't going to be in the family picture and then my Uncle Dick decided that he wasn't going to let that happen. Brennan is smiling—like a little kid. I like that. He put his head right on my shoulder.

My mom was doing like mother stuff—like in *Father of the Bride*—when the mother showed the son-in-law pictures of her daughter when she was a little girl. My mom was trying to make Brennan feel welcome in the family so she's showing him these very, very effeminate pictures of me dressing up in dresses when I was little. She was imitating me. Embarrassing!

My youngest brother, T.J., has no problem playing a joke on me or whoever I'm with. He's very accepting of whoever I bring home. He's really cool around gay people. He thinks they're fun. I mean, he'll wrestle with them, mess with them, play with them as if they were, you know—as if they were his brother.

I think Corey has more of a problem with me being gay. He doesn't talk about it, but it is obvious, you know, he'll just shake his head. He's a lot more like my dad. T.J. is very protective of me. I mean, he got suspended from school for beating a kid up because the kid said something about me. Corey is more shy and withdrawn and I think he gets a lot more embarrassed about the things people say about me.

I had something to prove not only to my family, but to everybody in town. My parents wanted me to be quiet. Part of it was protecting me, they didn't want me to get hurt. But part of it was their own embarrassment that I was gay. It was frustrating and I'd get angry and purposely do things because I knew it would make them mad. So part of it was, I should be able to do this, and part of it was, I'm going to do it because they say I can't. You know, the rebellion thing.

My dad would either blow up or he'd just keep it all inside and not say anything. A lot of times, I knew what he was feeling by his facial expressions, his body language, his erruh!—grunting straight noises—I don't know what else to call them.

He said things in a joking way, but he meant it. Stuff like "You going to wear your purse downtown?" or "Do you have to wear that damn thing? You damn faggot!" It was meant to say, "I really would rather you didn't do that." But the way he'd act—I'd do it just because.

I had a major explosion on the way back to the cities. Brennan and I argued about legalizing drugs—smoking marijuana. I was really upset. I was bawling. I've always had a deep hatred of alcohol and drugs. He said I had personal problems with it, because of my family. But for him it's like once every six months and it's like going to the zoo or whatever. The fact that he even smoked pot just drove me crazy.

I just won't handle it. There is no way. I don't have to and I won't. He promised me, he said that he would try. I let it go, because I was so in love . . . naive . . . about everything. I mean, how was I so stupid? I don't know how I didn't know that he cheated on me all those times. He'd call me and say, "I'm drunk and I'm going to stay over at this friend's house." How could I have been that dumb? I didn't want to see it.

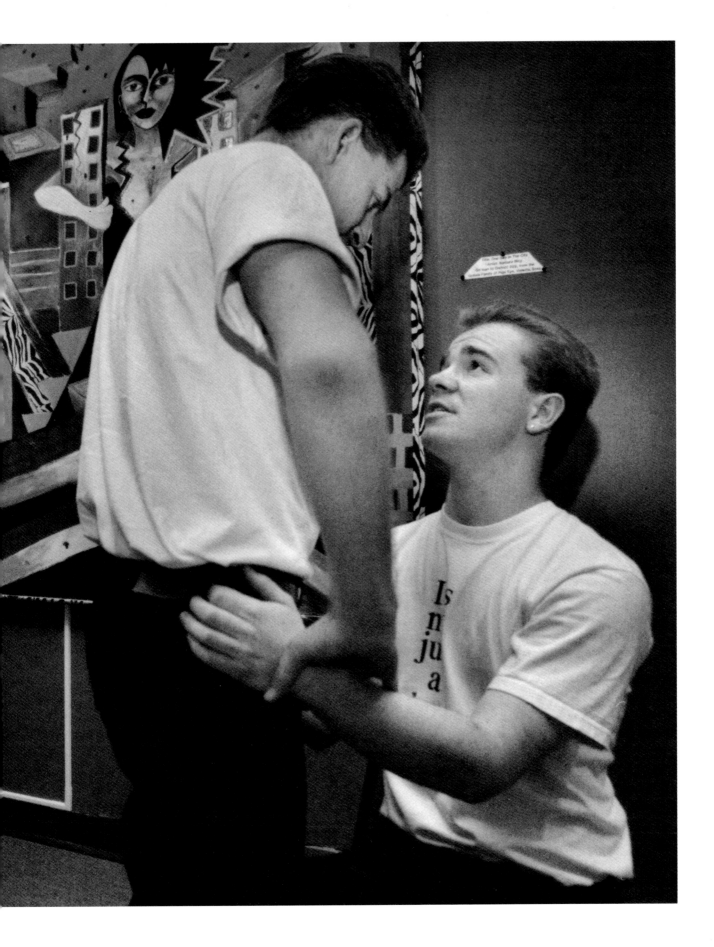

It is the end of my life, that's what it feels like anyway. I'm miserable. I can't quit crying. I'm sick at my stomach. I threw up three times last night. It's to the point where I want to hurt myself physically so I won't have to feel this pain anymore. I want to know why, dammit, why is he doing this to me? Why after telling me he loved me and then showing me for so long that he loved me, why say one day, "Well, I don't love you anymore"?

I'd be absolutely nuts if I didn't have my parents for security. I'm wishing I was a baby. People take care of you, love you and you don't even have to talk to them. This is the way I'm feeling right now. I want to say, "I don't care what you have to do, just make me feel like a baby."

I don't allow myself to get depressed anymore. I learned a lot. It will happen again. That was my first relationship, not my last.

I'm terrified of being alone. All of a sudden I find myself out on my own. It's really scary to think that my family isn't right here. I have to take care of myself. I want to throw myself at people so I don't have to face the fear.

This friend of mine called and I said, "I feel so alone."

He said, "You're not alone."

I said, "What do you mean?"

He said, "You have one of the strongest people I know with you."

I go, "What are you talking about?"

He said, "You."

I never think of myself as a strong person. I'm pretty strong, I have to be. Sometimes it just amazes me I keep going and going and going. I'm like the Energizer battery.

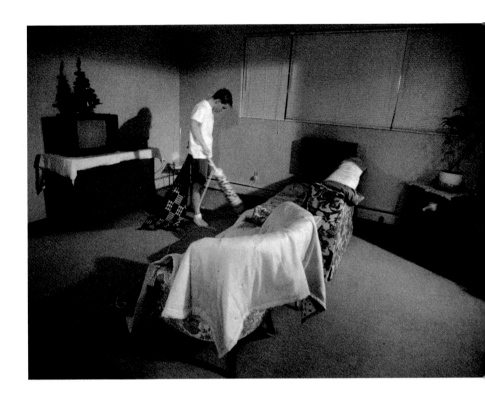

I'm a mac-and-cheese-add-water-and-boil kind of guy. That's how I grew up eating—we had a lot of Spam and mac and cheese and those Oriental meals in two cans that you put together, which I really like.

I hooked up with Lutheran Social Services back when I moved out of Luke and Steve's. So when I left Brennan's and started looking for an apartment, the social worker from before got me into a program that helped pay my rent and security deposit and got me all this furniture. They have a storage place where you go and take what you want. There wasn't much to choose from, but I took a lot. I just wanted a lot of furniture to fill up an apartment.

I found a picture of Martin Luther King—he's one of my heroes—him and Oprah Winfrey and Abraham Lincoln. I hope that I can do stuff to make a difference for the people who come after me. I think that's people's purpose in life and so I guess that's why I admire him and he's one of my role models.

Everybody's supposed to have a housewarming when they get a new apartment. We had Kool-Aid and egg salad sandwiches—lots of them. Jessey was in charge of the menu. I was in charge of cleaning—getting ready.

We watched the Three Stooges—no, it was Laurel and Hardy. It was one or the other because I find them both very hilarious. Me and Jessey are just Laurel and Hardy fans. Nobody else seemed to be, but all my friends were there.

I've done a lot of moving. I'm done. I'm tired of moving. I want to be settled—*big time!*

I got a job at District 202—the gay youth center . . . I hoped to help make it a good place for kids. We closed at midnight . . . so I was there till one o'clock cleaning up. By the end of every night, I felt tired and like nothing was changing . . . kids were always bickering and putting each other down.

I saw a lot of gay and lesbian kids, and they all wanted to be loved and accepted by someone, a boyfriend or an older person—someone who was going to take care of them. I mean, they wanted it from their family, but a lot of them weren't getting it.

A lot people did find it in 202. There was a group of us, you know, we all cared about each other—kind of took care of each other.

It would have been my senior year and I wanted to go to prom with a guy, so I decided that 202 should have a prom. We formed a committee and organized the first gay youth prom in the Twin Cities.

I wanted it to be perfect. We had black tails and canes and gloves and we got a convertible. We went to a very very expensive restaurant. Our appetizer was like fifteen dollars. We didn't even know what it was—so we didn't eat it. We looked at it.

I went with Ken, a guy I dated for a while. We had already broken up, but he knew how important it was to me. It was important to him, too. He went to his prom with a girl. I was sorry that our relationship never worked out. I felt kind of guilty about that. I do this dumb thing— I think if you date someone long enough, you eventually will be attracted to them. It just doesn't work that way. I really wished we had been boyfriends or that I could have gone to prom with a boyfriend.

I wanted to pretend like we were queens. People do that, you know, they wear their prom dress and stuff and ride around in a convertible.

Riding down Hennepin was really neat, because it's the gay street. It's like the downtown street of Minneapolis with all the lights and all the gay bars and clubs—and the Hennepin Avenue Bridge—I think it's probably the most beautiful in Minneapolis.

It represented kind of a normal youth experience. Everybody talks about their proms and what they remember and who they went with. I was taking back the high school experiences that I lost—making them my own.

I would really have liked to go to my home high school prom in Ashland with a guy—because that's the way I think things should have been instead of the way things were. I mean, I had to make a lot of things happen for me instead of just living through them. I had to make my adolescence. I had to make my youth. I had to take it back, you know.

Amy Grahn

Epilogue

Amy and Lizz's September reunion wasn't all that Amy had hoped. When Lizz returned to Minnesota for school she was preoccupied with her classes and in the throes of her own coming-out process. She pushed Amy away, pulled her back, then pushed her away again. Finally, they broke up, but for the next year, Amy carried a torch for Lizz. She couldn't get seriously interested in dating anyone else. Eventually she began to date a little, but admitted she was only filling her time, her emptiness.

Trying to stay positive and move forward with her life, Amy turned her attention to planning for the future. She considered enlisting in the military, but discovered her junior-high-era hospitalization for depression made her ineligible. She took a job as a teacher's aide in a day-care center to pay off the debts she had incurred while living on her own in the city and to save for a col-

lege program in law enforcement. Working at the day-care center for a year, she discovered she enjoyed working with children.

As her twenty-first birthday approached, Amy felt it was time to be on her own. She moved from her parents' home, left her day-care work, and took a job waiting tables in a gay bar. Within a couple of months of turning twenty-one, Amy packed up and left Minnesota, moving to Missouri to live with lesbian friends already there. She found work driving buses, first for the school district and eventually for the city.

At her first Gay Pride festival in Missouri, she met Rusty Ferrel and her five-year-old son, Michael. Amy asked Rusty out. Within a few months they were involved and talking about making a more serious commitment. On a romantic weekend getaway, Rusty proposed. The date was set, the rings purchased, the vows written, and

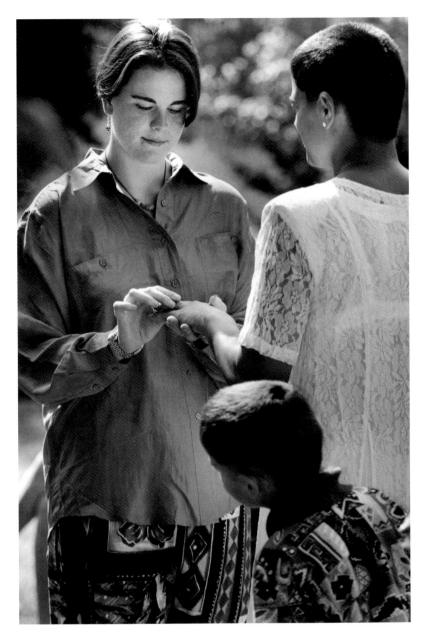

within a year of Amy's move, her family was on the road to Missouri for Amy and Rusty's commitment ceremony.

Amy and Rusty were wed at the Unitarian Universalist Church in Columbia, Missouri, on June 29, 1996. Michael was the ring bearer. Amy's brother, Chris, was her man of honor. It was Amy's grandparents' wedding anniversary. In August, Amy's mother, Sue, hosted a Minnesota reception for Rusty and Amy. The house and yard were filled with family and friends bestowing gifts and best wishes on the new couple.

Family, so important in Amy's life, now has added dimensions. Amy is determined to do her part in supporting her new family financially. When considering career options, she mentions taking the examination for a position as a city firefighter or going to college to study elementary education, psychology, or photojournalism. She has given up thoughts of becoming a police officer, saying the work is too dangerous for someone with a family. She relishes her role in parenting Michael. Amy and Rusty bought and moved into a three-bedroom home in Columbia in the fall of 1996. They share dreams of filling it with more children.

Jamie Nabozny

Epilogue

Prom couldn't assuage Jamie's grief over his lost senior year. Unable to both support himself and go to school, he took and passed the GED exams, earning the equivalent of a high school diploma. But Jamie felt it was a second-rate accomplishment. Neither of his parents had finished high school, and he had been looking forward to making them proud of him as the first of their three sons to graduate.

In the fall of 1993, at the start of what should have been his senior year, Jamie talked to an attorney about suing his school for damages and the right to graduate with his class. The lawyer took the case, giving Jamie hopes for a quick out-of-court settlement. It didn't happen, and the 1994 Ashland High School graduation came and went without him.

Jamie's attorney filed a complaint in federal court against the Ashland Public School District and individual school officials in

February 1995, claiming a violation of Jamie's constitutional rights of equal protection and due process. The federal district court in Madison, Wisconsin, dismissed the case without trial in October.

Jamie accepted an offer from Lambda Legal Defense and Education Fund to appeal that ruling. Lambda, a lesbian and gay legal organization, uses test-case litigation to defend and extend the civil rights of lesbians, gay men, and people with HIV/AIDS. Jamie's case, as the first to challenge antigay violence in public schools, offered the opportunity to set precedent.

Lambda attorney David Buckel invited Jamie to Washington, D.C., for a press conference and lobbying on Capitol Hill. Jamie's

father, Bob, accompanied him. It was a big day for Jamie; his fight against injustice had reached a national stage, and his father was finally and unconditionally at his side.

Lambda argued the appeal, *Nabozny* v. *Podlesny*, before the Seventh Circuit Court of Appeals in Chicago in March 1996. On July 31, the appeals court reversed the lower court's decision and ruled that under the Equal Protection Clause of the United States Constitution, Jamie could sue the Ashland Public School District and school officials individually for monetary damages over their failure to address the antigay abuse he suffered at the hands of other students. Although binding only in the three states of the Seventh Circuit, the ruling is seen as precedent and considered persuasive for courts throughout the country. It is heralded as a victory for gay and lesbian students nationwide, because it puts school officials on notice that not only the district but they personally may be held liable if they fail to address antigay harassment and abuse in their schools.

On November 19, 1996, a federal jury in Eau Claire, Wisconsin, sided with Jamie, finding two Ashland school principals and one assistant principal liable for not protecting Jamie from abuse by other students. The school settled with Jamie for nearly $1 million. Jamie hopes to start college in the fall of 1997 in pursuit of a degree in psychology and counseling. He dreams of founding a group home—a safe place that gay and lesbian teens fleeing small-town prejudices can call home.

Bibliography

Bell, A., and Weinberg, M. *Homosexualities: A Study of Diversity Among Men and Women*. New York: Simon and Schuster, 1978.

Bell, A., Weinberg, M., and Hammersmith, S. *Sexual Preference: Its Development in Men and Women*. Bloomington: Indiana University Press, 1981.

Berrill, K. "Anti-Gay Violence and Victimization in the United States." *Journal of Interpersonal Violence* 5, no. 3 (September 1990): 274–94.

Burr, C. "Homosexuality and Biology." *Atlantic Monthly*, March 1993, pp. 47–65.

Gibson, P. "Gay Male and Lesbian Youth Suicide," in *Report of the Secretary's Task Force on Youth Suicide*. Pub. No. (ADM) 89–1623. Washington, D.C.: U.S. Department of Health and Human Services, 1989.

Hunter, J. "Violence Against Lesbian and Gay Male Youths." *Journal of Interpersonal Violence* 5, no. 3 (September 1990): 295–300.

Hunter, J., and Schaecher, R. "Stresses on Lesbian and Gay Adolescents in Schools." *Social Work in Education* 9, no. 3 (Spring 1987): 180–89.

Jay, K., and Young, A. *The Gay Report: Lesbians and Gay Men Speak Out About Their Sexual Experiences and Lifestyles*. New York: Summit, 1977.

Making Schools Safe for Gay and Lesbian Youth: Breaking the Silence in Schools and in Families. Education Report, Governor's Commission on Gay and Lesbian Youth, Commonwealth of Massachusetts. 1993.

Martin, A. D., and Hetrick, E. S. "The Stigmatization of the Gay and Lesbian Adolescent." *Journal of Homosexuality* 15, no. 1–2, (1988): 163–83.

Reed, R., and Chandler, K. "Growing Up Gay: A Crisis in Hiding." *Star Tribune*, Special Section, Dec. 6, 1992.

Remafedi, G. "Adolescent Homosexuality: Psychosocial and Medical Implications." *Pediatrics* 79, no. 3 (March 1987): 331–37.

Remafedi, G. "Homosexual Youth: A Challenge to Contemporary Society." *Journal of the American Medical Association* 258, no. 2 (July 1987): 222–25.

Remafedi, G. "Male Homosexuality: The Adolescent's Perspective." *Pediatrics* 79, no. 3 (March 1987): 326–30.

Remafedi, G., Resnick, M., Blum, R., and Harris, L. "Demography of Sexual Orientation in Adolescents." *Pediatrics* 89, no. 4 (April 1992): 714–21.

Savin-Williams, R. C. "Theoretical Perspectives Accounting for Adolescent Homosexuality." *Journal of Adolescent Health Care* 9, no. 2 (March 1988): 95–104.

Troiden, R. R. "Homosexual Identity Development." *Journal of Adolescent Health Care* 9, no. 2 (March 1988): 105–13.

Uribe, V. and Harbeck, K. M. "Addressing the Needs of Lesbian, Gay, and Bisexual Youth: The Origins of PROJECT 10 and School-Based Interventions." In K. M. Harbeck, ed., *Coming out of the Classroom Closet: Gay and Lesbian Students, Teachers and Curricula*, pp. 9–28. New York: Haworth Press, 1992.

Whitlock, K. *Bridges of Respect: Creating Support for Lesbian and Gay Youth*. 2nd ed. Philadelphia: American Friends Service Committee, 1989.

Recommended Reading

Aarons, Leroy. *Prayers for Bobby: A Mother's Coming to Terms with the Suicide of Her Gay Son*. San Francisco: HarperCollins, 1995.
A moving account of Mary Griffith's personal journey and examination of her faith after her gay son, Bobby, committed suicide at the age of twenty. Includes excerpts from the journal in which Bobby recorded his inner struggles.

Balka, Christie, and Rose, Andy, eds. *Twice Blessed: On Being Gay and Jewish*. Boston: Beacon Press, 1989.
This is the first anthology of essays by and about lesbian and gay Jews maintaining their ties to Jewish tradition while celebrating their gay pride.

Bass, Ellen, and Kaufman, Kate. *Free Your Mind: The Book for Gay, Lesbian and Bisexual Youth–and Their Allies*. New York: HarperCollins, 1996.
An encyclopedic guidebook for gay youth and adults who care about them with emphasis on self-acceptance and a resourceful celebration of life. Includes the voices of a diverse group of young people and practical advice on issues of concern to them.

Beam, Joseph, ed. *In the Life: A Black Gay Anthology*. Boston: Alyson Publications, 1986.
A compilation of works by African-American authors exploring their role and status as a double minority in present-day America.

Bernstein, Robert A. *Straight Parents Gay Children: Keeping Families Together*. New York: Thunder's Mouth Press, 1995.
A father's personal account of his coming to terms with a daughter's sexual orientation and his experiences with P-FLAG, an organization that helps parents keep families together and speaks out on behalf of their gay children.

Brelin, Christa, ed. *Strength in Numbers: A Lesbian, Gay and Bisexual Resource*. New York: Visible Ink Press, 1996.
A comprehensive listing of resources and information cross-referenced by topics of interest and geographic location. Includes a substantial section especially for gay, lesbian, bisexual, and transgender youth with listings of resources, programs, and support groups.

Chandler, Kurt. *Passages of Pride: Lesbian and Gay Youth Come of Age*. New York: Random House, 1995.
A well-researched and well-written journalist's account of six teenagers' passage through the coming-out process. Includes information and insights from experts and parents.

Jennings, Kevin, ed. *Becoming Visible: A Reader in Gay and Lesbian History for High School and College Students*. Boston: Alyson Publications, 1994.
Readings in the history of many cultures over the span of two thousand years. Includes study questions, class activities, and primary and secondary sources.

Grahn, Judy. *Another Mother Tongue*. Boston: Beacon Press, 1990.
An engagingly witty mix of history and autobiography that celebrates gay culture.

Rafkin, Louise. *Different Daughters: A Book by Mothers of Lesbians*. Pittsburgh: Cleis Press, 1996.
Honest voices of twenty-six mothers speaking about their feelings, love, and challenges in coming to terms with a daughter's lesbianism. Valuable insights for those just starting on this journey.

Remafedi, Gary, ed. *Death by Denial: Studies of Suicide in Gay and Lesbian Teenagers*. Boston: Alyson Publications, 1994.
A research collection documenting the problems gay and lesbian teenagers face in coming out. Includes the hard-to-find 1989 federal suicide study and others.

Singer, Bennett L., ed. *Growing Up Gay / Growing Up Lesbian: A Literary Anthology*. New York: New Press, 1994.
Collection of fiction, poetry, and essays from known authors, celebrities, and gay youth.

Resources

Someone to talk to:

1-800-347-TEEN
National Gay/Lesbian/Bisexual Youth
Hotline—Indianapolis
Thurs.–Sun. 7–10 p.m. EST, Fri.–Sat. 7
p.m.–midnight EST

1-800-96-YOUTH
The OutYouth Austin Helpline
Daily 5:30–9:30 p.m. CST

National Runaway Switchboard
1-800-621-4000
1-800-621-0394 (hearing-impaired)
24 hours a day, 7 days a week

National AIDS Hotline (run by
the Center for Disease Control)
1-800-342-AIDS (English)
1-800-344-SIDA (Spanish)
1-800-243-7889 (hearing-impaired)
HIV/AIDS information, 24 hours a
day, 7 days a week

Letter Exchange
Alyson Publications
40 Plympton St.
Boston, MA 02118
For those 21 and under, no charge. Write
a letter and the exchange trades it for
another.

Making local connections:

Bridges Project of the National Youth
Advocacy Coalition
1711 Connecticut Ave. NW, Suite 206
Washington, D.C. 20009-1139
Phone: 202-319-7596
Fax: 202-319-7365
E-mail: NYouthAC@ aol.com
Provides information, referrals, and
resources on issues affecting gay, lesbian,
bisexual, and transgender youth. With its
move to Washington, D.C., it adds advocacy and public policy to its activities.
Maintains a database of 5,000 entries and
will mail or fax information and print
and audiovisual materials. Publishes
Crossroads, a national newsletter with
items of interest to youth.

Lambda Youth Network
P.O. 7911, Culver City, CA 90233
E-mail: lambdayn@aol.com
For a list of lesbian, gay, and bisexual
youth groups, youth newsletters, pen
pal programs, community centers, and
P-FLAG chapters in your area, send a
large self-addressed envelope with two
stamps and $1. The service requires that

you state your age and where you heard
about LYN.

National Gay Youth Network (NGYN)
P.O. Box 846
San Francisco, CA 94101-0846
Composed of gay youth groups, gay
student unions, and sponsors, this net-
working group publishes the *Gay Youth
Community News* and the *We Are Here
Guide*, offering state-by-state resources.
It also publishes information on how to
start a youth group in your area.

!OutProud!, National Coalition for Gay,
Lesbian, and Bisexual & Transgender
Youth
P.O. Box 24589, San Jose, CA 95154-4589
E-mail: info@outproud.org
Resource guide for youth and educators
with topics like news, activism, litera-
ture, and school resources. Its national
database, *QueerAmerica*, serves as referral
source of local resources for lesbian,
gay, and bisexual teens and a materials
source to youth-service providers.
Internet access.

Making on-line connections:

America Online
Gay and Lesbian Community Forum: key-
word GAY. Go to Discussion Boards and
then to Gay Message Board—Teens Talk,
or to Lesbian Message Board—Baby
Dykes, or to Bisexual Message Board—
Bisexual Teens.

World Wide Web
Information, resource lists, and people
to talk to can be found on the Internet
and the WWW. Since addresses and
URLs change quickly, use your favorite
search engine to search gay, lesbian, and
bisexual youth or look under the names
of one of the following: *!OutProud!*,
*Oasis, The Queer Resources Directory,
ELIGHT, infoqueer, InsideOut*

For parents, educators and other adults:

P-FLAG (Parents, Families, and Friends
of Lesbians and Gays)
1101 14th Street NW, Suite 1030
Washington, D.C. 20005
Phone: 202-638-4200
Email: info@PFLAG.org
A national parents' organization offering
help, support, education, and advocacy
for gays and lesbians and their parents,
siblings, and friends. Over 410 chapters
nationwide.

Gay, Lesbian and Straight Teachers
Network (GLSTN)
122 W. 26th St., Suite 1100
New York, NY 10001
Phone: 212-727-0135
Fax: 212-727-0254
E-mail: GLSTN@glstn.org
A national organization of teachers with
chapters throughout the nation. Offers
resources and help for parents, teachers,
and schools on the World Wide Web
under GLSTN Toolbox. Also sponsors a
national "Back to School" campaign.

PROJECT 10
7850 Melrose Avenue
Los Angeles, CA 90046
Phone: 213-651-5200 or 818-577-4553
Nation's oldest school support program.
Handbook and video available.

National Youth Advocacy Coalition
1711 Connecticut Ave. NW, Suite 206
Washington, D.C. 20009-1139
Phone: 202-319-7596
Fax: 202-319-7365
E-mail: NYouthAC@aol.com
Sponsored by the Hetrick-Martin
Institute. Addresses public policy issues
related to gay, lesbian, bisexual, and
transgender youth by coordinating col-
laboration between national and commu-
nity-based organizations, both gay-
specific and mainstream. Serves as a
referral source and a clearinghouse for
the latest information on lesbian and gay
youth issues.

Hetrick-Martin Institute
2 Astor Place
New York, NY 10003-6998
Phone: 212-674-2400
Fax: 212-674-8650
TTY: 212-674-8695
The oldest and largest agency serving
gay, lesbian, and bisexual youth.
Provides education for youth service
agencies and the public about the needs
of gay and lesbian youth, and direct ser-
vices to youth in New York, including
running the Harvey Milk School.
Publishes a national directory, *You Are
Not Alone: National Directory of Lesbian,
Gay and Bisexual Youth Organizations*, and
a comic book series, *Tales of the Closet*.